EARTH'S LAST FRONTIERS

MOUNTAIN TOPS

Ellen Labrecque

Raintree is an imprint of Capstone Global Library Limited, a company incorporated in England and Wales having its registered office at 7 Pilgrim Street, London, EC4V 6LB – Registered company number: 6695582

www.raintreepublishers.co.uk
myorders@raintreepublishers.co.uk

Text © Capstone Global Library Limited 2014
First published in hardback in 2014
Paperback edition first published in 2015
The moral rights of the proprietor have been asserted.

Edited by Rebecca Rissman, Dan Nunn, and Adrian Vigliano
Designed by Tim Bond
Picture research by Liz Alexander
Originated by Capstone Global Library Ltd
Printed in China by CTPS

ISBN 978 1 406 27169 0 (hardback)
17 16 15 14 13
10 9 8 7 6 5 4 3 2 1

ISBN 978 1 406 27174 4 (paperback)
18 17 16 15 14
10 9 8 7 6 5 4 3 2 1

British Library Cataloguing in Publication Data
Labrecque, Ellen.
Mountain tops. – (Earth's last frontiers)
A full catalogue record for this book is available from the British Library.

Acknowledgements
We would like to thank the following for permission to reproduce photographs:

Brad Wilson, DVM p. 23; Corbis pp. 13 (© Galen Rowell), 14 (© Jerry Kobalenko/First Light), 18 (© Reza/Webistan), 19 (© Anatoly Maltsev/epa), 22 (© Martin Harvey), 25 (© Ocean), 24 (© Konrad Wothe/Minden Pictures), 26 (© François Pugnet/Kipa), 29 (© Russ Heinl/All Canada Photos); Getty Images pp. 6 (Jonathan Barton), 7 (Sergio Cruz Photography), 8 (Tim Laman /National Geographic), 10 (© Rory O'Bryen 2010), 21 (Universal History Archive); NASA p. 4; Nature Picture Library pp. 15 (© Bryan and Cherry Alexander), 17 (© Freya Pratt); Press Association Images p. 11 (BLANCA HUERTAS/AP); Shutterstock pp. 5 (© Dominik Michalek), 9 (© Zvonimir Atletic), 20 (© Volodymyr Goinyk), 27 (© Rechitan Sorin), 28 (© vichie81); SuperStock pp. 12 (LatitudeStock), 16 (StockTrek Images); Design features courtesy of Shutterstock (© sabri deniz kizil).

Cover photograph of Dolomites, Italy reproduced with permission of Superstock (Fritz Breig / Mauritius).

Every effort has been made to contact copyright holders of material reproduced in this book. Any omissions will be rectified in subsequent printings if notice is given to the publisher.

All the internet addresses (URLs) given in this book were valid at the time of going to press. However, due to the dynamic nature of the internet, some addresses may have changed, or sites may have changed or ceased to exist since publication. While the author and publisher regret any inconvenience this may cause readers, no responsibility for any such changes can be accepted by either the author or the publisher.

CONTENTS

A FINAL FRONTIER

Even though more than seven billion people live on Earth, there are still places left to explore! Some of Earth's mountain tops are very difficult to reach. Let's take a look at some of these unexplored peaks.

WOW!

People who climb mountains for the sport of it are called mountaineers. Mount Everest is the world's highest mountain at 8,848 metres (29,029 feet). About 1,500 people have climbed it.

WHAT ARE MOUNTAIN TOPS?

Mountains can be found on every **continent** and even under the ocean. They are found in many of the world's countries. A mountain can stand alone with just one peak or **summit**, the mountain top. Or it can be part of a whole row of mountains called a **mountain range**.

WOW!

The longest mountain range on land is the Andes. It stretches along the west coast of South America and has many unexplored peaks.

WHY ARE MOUNTAIN TOPS UNEXPLORED?

Unpredictable weather makes it dangerous for people to explore mountain tops. Storms can appear without warning. Cold temperatures, snow, and wind can be life-threatening at the top of a mountain.

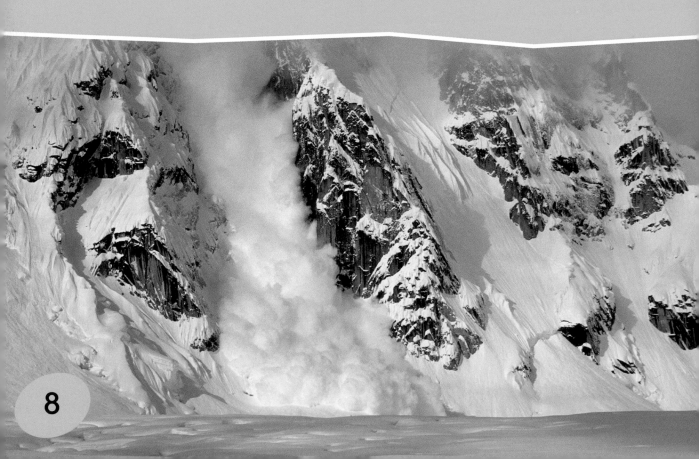

WOW!

Mountain tops take your breath away… Really! The higher you climb, the harder it is to breathe.

DANGEROUS MOUNTAINS

Some mountain tops in the Yariguíes range in Colombia are still unexplored. Violent wars in the area and dense forests kept explorers away for years.

WOW!

In 2006, brave explorers safely travelled by helicopter to one of the peaks of the Yariguíes range. While there, the scientists discovered a bird that had never been seen before!

SACRED MOUNTAINS

Gangkhar Puensum, in Bhutan, is the highest unclimbed mountain. It is 7,570 metres (24,836 feet) above sea level. Local people believe the mountain top is home to spirits who should not be disturbed.

WOW!

Mount Kailash in Western China (Tibet) has never been climbed. Four different religious groups consider it the world's holiest mountain.

TOP OF THE WORLD

Some mountain tops in the cold and dark Arctic region have never been seen. Some of them have never even been named. They are surrounded by ice and they would be too hard and dangerous to reach.

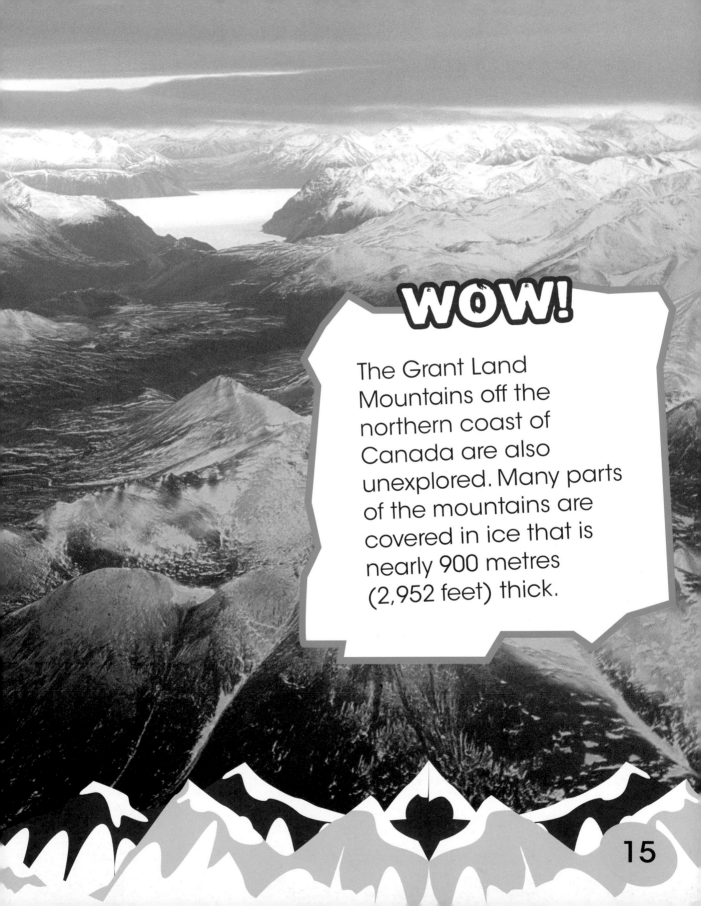

WOW!

The Grant Land Mountains off the northern coast of Canada are also unexplored. Many parts of the mountains are covered in ice that is nearly 900 metres (2,952 feet) thick.

BOTTOM OF THE WORLD

Mountain tops in the Andes mountain range at the bottom of South America are still **unconquered**. The weather is very unpredictable in this region. Wild windstorms, known as the williwaw, appear out of nowhere.

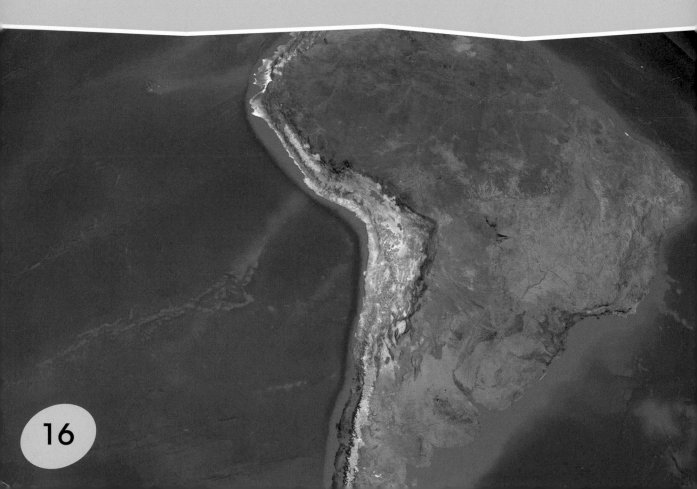

WOW!

Amazing animals, such as this puma, can be found in the tiny Quimsa Cruz range in Bolivia. Few people have explored these mountains because they are very difficult to reach.

ROOF OF THE WORLD

The Pamir Mountains of Tajikistan are the least visited mountains in the world. Locals call the area "the Roof of the World". These mountains are some of the world's highest.

WOW!

Explorers have to deal with very sudden weather changes on the Pamir Mountains. **Avalanches** and flash floods happen quickly without any warning.

UNDER SEA AND ICE

The Gamburtsev Mountains are a long mountain range in East Antarctica. They are believed to be about 2,700 metres (8,900 feet) high. But they are completely covered by 600 metres (2,000 feet) of ice.

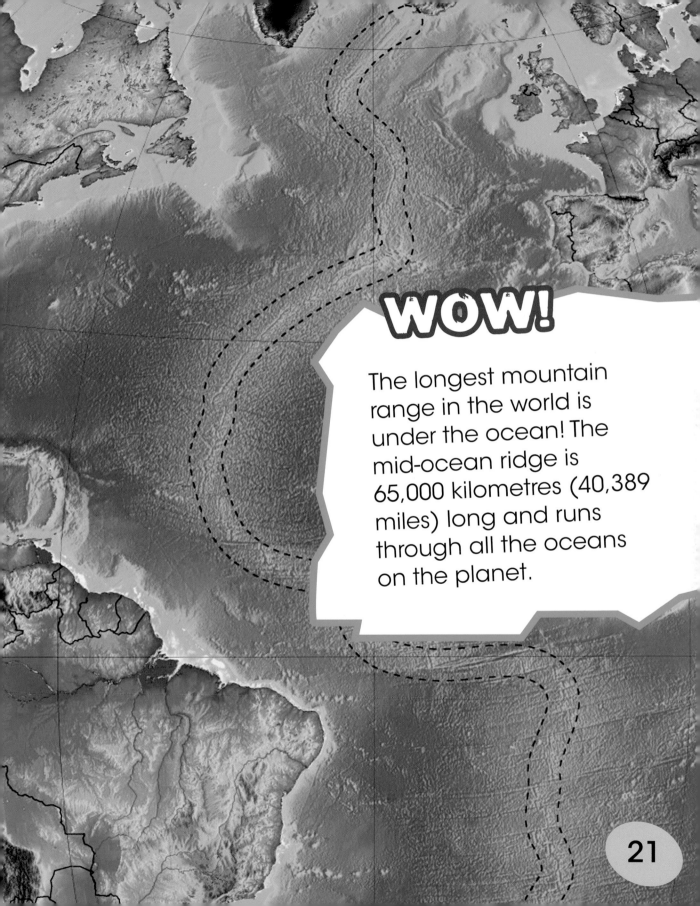

WOW!

The longest mountain range in the world is under the ocean! The mid-ocean ridge is 65,000 kilometres (40,389 miles) long and runs through all the oceans on the planet.

CROWDED IN THE SKY

Tepuis are table-top mountains found in the Amazon rainforest in South America. To reach the towering tops, explorers have to scale dangerous cliffs or fly in on a helicopter.

WOW!

Species found on the top of tepuis are found nowhere else in the world. The flat tops of these mountains are like islands in the sky filled with rare and unusual creatures.

NEW MOUNTAIN TOP SPECIES

New plants and animals are still being discovered today. The world's largest moth was discovered on Mount Kinabalu on the island of Borneo in 2012. Its wingspan is 30 centimetres (12 inches) long.

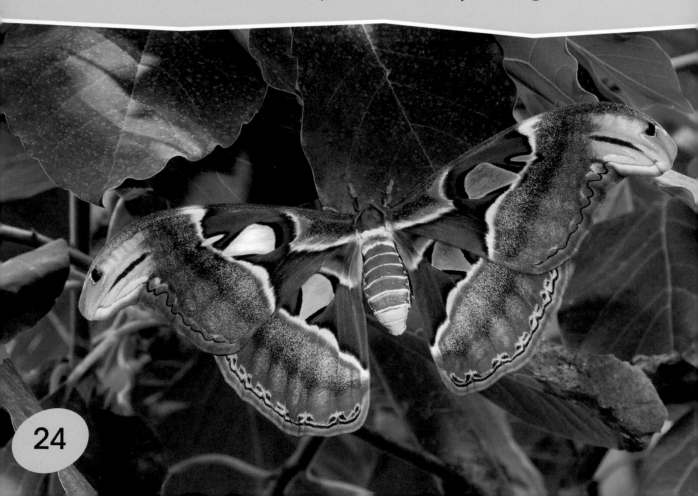

WOW!

There could be many other undiscovered plants and animals living on this towering mountain!

HOW WE EXPLORE

Technology has made exploring mountain tops easier than ever. Scientists can take helicopters to the peaks. Satellite phones help climbers call for help if they need it.

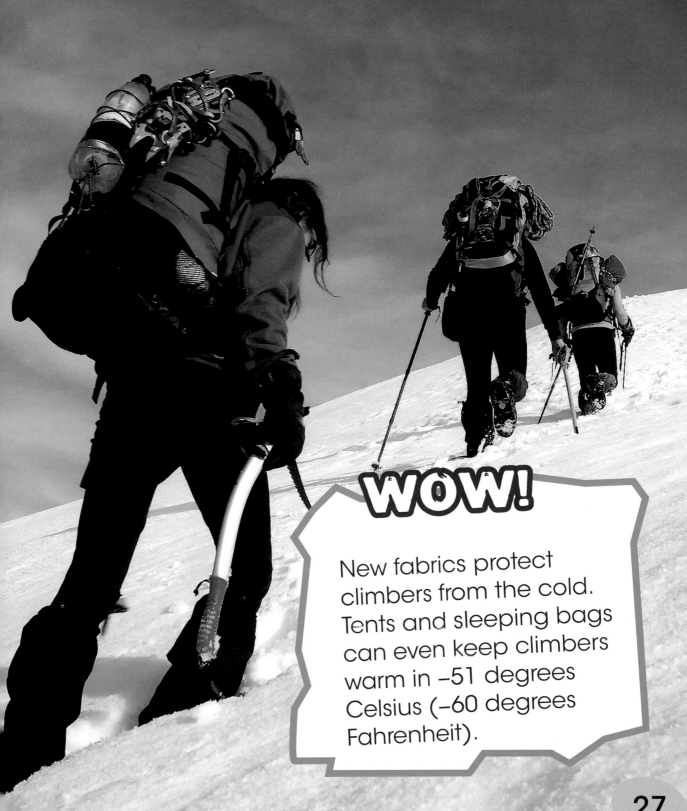

WOW!

New fabrics protect climbers from the cold. Tents and sleeping bags can even keep climbers warm in −51 degrees Celsius (−60 degrees Fahrenheit).

ONLY ON THE MOUNTAINS

Mountain tops look **majestic**. But they are also places with dangerous **climates**. Many explorers have died trying to reach the tops of the world's highest mountains.

Extreme conditions on mountain tops mean there are many unexplored peaks. One day, explorers may be able to reach every summit.

GLOSSARY

avalanche wave of snow, ice, and rocks that slides quickly down a mountain

climate what the weather is like in an area over a long time

continent seven biggest land masses on Earth, including Africa, Antarctica, Asia, Australasia, Europe, North America, and South America

majestic impressive beauty

mountain range long chain of mountains

species living organisms that are very similar to each other and can reproduce

summit highest point of a hill or mountain

unconquered not climbed or overcome

FIND OUT MORE

There are lots of sources with information about mountains! You can start with these books and websites.

BOOKS

Mountains, Margaret Hynes (Kingfisher, 2007)

Mountains (Geography Corner), Ruth Thomson (Wayland, 2011)

Mountains (Go Facts: Natural Environments), Ian Rohr (A&C Black, 2009)

WEBSITES

www.bbc.co.uk/nature/habitats/Mountain
See some amazing videos about mountains on the BBC's nature website.

www.sciencekids.co.nz/sciencefacts/earth/mounteverest.html
Learn more about Mount Everest, the world's highest mountain.

INDEX